PORTRAIT of POLPERRO

Sheila de Burlet

An aerial view of Polperro in the 1970s showing the inlet in the coast which provided a haven and led to the development of the fishing village

In 1871, Thomas Quiller Couch edited his father's notes and published *The History of Polperro*, one of the best local histories, but since that time a wealth of information has become available and it is this which has formed the framework for this book. It has had to be extracted from a wide variety of sources: from ancient deeds, legal documents, Acts of Parliament, naval and army records, farm leases, parish registers, churchwarden's accounts, tithe records, wills, election papers, newspapers and many more.

Polperro is a 13th century fishing village, lying in a rock-bound gap in the coastline, 15 miles south-west of the estuary of the River Tamar. In Cornish its name means porth - a harbour, the second element may be a river name but this is uncertain. The village lies in two parishes: Lansallos and Talland, and has an intriguing and often exciting history. Today, it is one of the most beautiful places in the country, visited by hundreds and thousands of tourists. This book is written both for them, and for those fortunate enough to live in Polperro all the year round.

The unwritten records

If we look at the air photograph of the area inland from Polperro, we see walled fields and isolated farmhouses. This is a long-inhabited landscape and is largely the work of man. It is a record of centuries of sustained work and planning during which the land was altered by human habitation and human needs. The area is well watered and traversed by narrow lanes that have been trackways ever since prehistoric man settled in this part of Cornwall.

As soon as Cornish walls are built, they are adopted by nature. In colder regions the walls remain bare but in the milder climate they are one of the glories of the Cornish landscape, covered as they are with ferns, mosses, woodsage, and topped by ash, oak, holly and hazel. In spring the countryside around Polperro is softened by thick white clouds of blackthorn in blossom. Roadside verges are smothered in bluebells, or primroses buttoned into the grass banks.

The natural rock gardens along the cliffs to east and west of the harbour are covered in pink thrift and gorse has colonised the old potato gardens. In May, the early purple orchid appears in the banks, dark rose-purple, with tiny sepals spreading out to the sun, toning perfectly with outcrops of old red sandstone.

Hundreds of sites called 'rounds' are found in Cornwall, and date from the Iron Age (550 BC) and Romano-British times (45 AD) and the first known habitation site at Polperro is the Round Field at Talland Hill. This site was well chosen as it lay below the prevailing wind and had a good water supply from the stream that flows down Pallace Schute to the harbour. The Round Field is over an acre in size but there is nothing visible on the ground to show the huts and cooking places. A find by the late Ralph Penter in 1955 on Talland Hill of six silver Roman coins was identified as double denari, all minted in Rome in about 237 AD. This does not mean that Romans lived in the area, but taken with other small finds it could mean that Roman coins circulated in normal trading practices. The so-called 'Roman' bridge was not built until 1870 and 'Saxon' Bridge replaced an earlier wooden structure.

The area around Polperro has been farmed since the Bronze Age, which began in Cornwall before 2000 BC, but few traces from this period remain in the two parishes, although several magnificent barrows can be seen at the Taphouses, while the Iron Age fort on Bury Down at Lanreath can be seen for miles. In the same way as vegetation grows on walls, burial barrows become clothed in green, hiding the art of the ancient builders. Mable Barrow in Lansallos was the burial place of an important Celt - it was a spread bowl barrow, like an inverted pudding bowl, but is now almost ploughed out. The site at Pennant (meaning 'top of the valley') may also have been the burial place of other Celts - the two adjacent fields are called Great and Little Burrow Parks and cover fourteen acres. The road from Mable Burrow leads to Landaviddy or nant-an-bethow, possibly meaning the 'valley of the graves'.

In Bronze Age burials the cremated remains were placed in a pottery urn and there was a long-standing belief in the Polperro locality that anyone finding such an urn should break it and hide the pieces. if such a relic was taken into a house it was said that the person whose ashes it contained would haunt the house and the people in it.

The prehistoric custom of erecting standing stones dates from Bronze Age times, possibly to mark important graves, and our modern gravestones may be a continuity of this ancient tribute to the dead. A huge standing stone (now fallen) lies at Kilminorth, just outside the curious round called, variously, the Wedding Ring, the Camp, or the Warren. The site is encircled by a magnificent wall, very old and well-preserved, but there are no traces of huts inside and it remains undated and something of a mystery. Early in the 19th century, Thomas Bond, the historian of Looe, saw several instruments of 'brass' (probably bronze) which were found at Kilminorth and Little Larnick, but all were sold to a buyer of scrap metal from Dock (Devonport) who hawked the countryside. Included amongst this priceless treasure was a gold chain tied to a stick to drive the cows. The little girl who found them told Bond that they were things which warriors used in ancient times.

An 1813 engraving showing Polperro viewed from the south. In keeping with the conventions of the time, the setting has been romanticised and exaggerated.

Activity on the fish quay at Polperro around 1900.

Fortunately, not all has been lost. The now famous Mycenean dagger and sword, both found in barrows in Pelynt, are in the County Museum in Truro. That they are there is due to Dr Jonathan Couch of Polperro. On a January day in 1835 he was paying a visit to a patient in Pelynt, and someone told him that a farmer had moved a bed of stones in the Five Barrow Field, so he went to the site and identified the remains of a cremation. The farmer had also found a piece of corroded metal which was not in the cavity of the bones. "The piece of metal," Couch wrote, "was evidently the remains of a spear, being of that shape.... on cutting it appears hard and shines like brass."

THE GIANT'S HEDGE

An unexplained feature of the Polperro area is the long but now interrupted stretch of linear earthwork and ditch stretching for eleven miles from West Looe Down to Lerryn on the Fowey river and called the Giant's Hedge - the only formation of its kind in Cornwall. Most of the earthworks in Britain were built after the Romans departed, and several, whose purpose is long forgotten but which are too large to be completely destroyed were credited to the Devil or to a race of giants.

A giant, having nothing else to do
Built a hedge from Lerryn to Looe

There has been, and still is, much speculation about the curious earth rampart. In 1830, Jonathan Couch saw it 'near perfect' on West Looe Downs and wrote that later this part of the earthwork was demolished and field walls built. It is neither a parochial boundary nor a manorial boundary, and the earliest description of it was by William Borlase, Rector of Ludgvan, when he described it in his excursion pocket book written up between 1751 and 1758. Part of the ditch and bank can still be seen at Hall Farm in Pelynt and in Willake Wood the ditch is twenty feet wide; at Ribby above Lerryn the bank is in good condition - over six feet wide at the top. To build this huge earthwork must have absorbed much time and labour, so it was presumably of enormous importance at the time of its construction. Dr Radford, in his 'Arthurian Sites in the West' speculates that it formed part of the boundary and defence of the estate or demense of King Mark.

THE EARLY INDEPENDENT YEARS

Cornwall remained independent until conquered by the English in 814 AD. It seems likely that prior to this date, the Cornish living in what became Lansallos parish set the basic patterns of life which continued for centuries thereafter. Fishermen had to live near their boats, always at risk from storms, while the farming families cleared more woodlands for pasture and arable farming. The isolated 'trefs' (homesteads) date from before the Norman conquest; names like Tregemelyn, Tregavithic, Trenewan. All are Cornish place names indicating the 'tref' of a person whose name is now lost, or a descriptive place name like Tregue - the farm in the hollow - or Tresquite, the farm by the wood.

Nothing is known of what happened when the English first came to Lansallos and Talland, or how their landowners dispossessed the Cornish Celts. Perhaps they took over the farms as going concerns based on the early system which we now call feudal. All that *is* certain about this period is what is written in the Domesday Book. Polperro itself is not mentioned, but it is recorded that an Englishwoman named Aelfeva held the manor of Raphael, Aelmar the Englishman held Lansallos manor, Edwi held Tregamellyn. By 1086, in their turn, the English were swept away and replaced by the Norman magnates.

Off to sea. The Polperro fishing fleet sets sail at the end of the 19th century.

The fishing haven
1303-1894

After the Domesday Book three new manors were established between the river at Polperro and West Looe, and were in the possession of Norman Frenchmen - Porthbyghan, Portlooe and Killigarth. The boundaries of the ancient Raphael manor were probably fixed before 1066 and took in the whole of Polperro harbour, extending well into Talland parish and covering every possible landing place. The road from Crumplehorn hamlet to Polperro formed its boundary and it included Fore Street, Talland Hill, Kit Hill, the cottage called Head O'Ditch and the Schute.

Raphael and Lansallos manors, two great estates comprising many farms, mills, woods, downlands, arable and pasture land, came into the possession of the Huish family in the 13th century. For at least five generations they lived at their manor house, Raphael itself, where they had their own private chapel licenced by the Bishop of Exeter.

Polperro was now important enough to be called upon to make its contribution to the war being waged by King Edward I against the Scots, and even remote settlements were ordered to supply men and ships to serve in the north. Officers, knights, bannerets, men at arms, seamen, archers, crossbowmen - all were required. It was in this connection that the first known written record of Polperro itself appeared. It was dated 10th April 1303, when a king's messenger was sent from Nottinghamshire where the king was en route to Scotland, and read:

"Request to the good men of Liskerit, Donheverd and Portpir (Liskeard, Launceston, Polperro) to aid the bailiffs and good men of the towns of Loo, Porthbygan and Assh (East and West Looe and Saltash) who at the king's request have granted a ship furnished with men and necessaries for serving against the Scots and to contribute to the expenses, as the King is informed by Gervaise Athelard, Admiral of the Fleet for those parts because the last mentioned towns cannot suffice to the expenses without the aid of the force, and the king sets great store by the expedition."

The request to the 'good men' of Polperro and elsewhere was not as polite as it sounds, because any Cornishman who refused to serve his king was to be locked up in Launceston Castle.

Polperro harbour was becoming a valuable source of income to the lords of Raphael and it remained privately owned until an Act of Parliament in 1894 vested the harbour in a body of trustees. In the same way that parking fees are collected today from motorists, the owners of Raphael collected fees from boat owners and traders. Money had to be paid for landing fish, on goods going in and out, and the steward or bailiff would be responsible for collecting money for anchorage, towage, keelage, ballastage and wharfage. In return, the landowners paid for the upkeep of the piers and quays. By the 14th century, fishing had become a specialised occupation for settled Cornish communities. The Black Prince's register contains many demands for fish for his army in Gascony, as well as his large private households, and the Polperro fishermen soon became rich enough to build their own chapel, near the Peak. It was licenced by the Bishop of Exeter in 1391 and dedicated to Saint Peter, the patron saint of fishermen, whose feast day was 10th July.

ABOVE: A very rare photograph taken inside the fish store owned by the Italian Teglio brothers and dating from the early 1900s.
BELOW: A sketch by Jonathan Couch in about 1840 of Polperro fishermen at work. Note the master seaner signalling with his hat.

For nearly 500 years, that day was always set aside for feast and fair days, the holy day gradually merging into a holiday. The chapel itself was used for a mere hundred and fifty years. Richard Couch, born in 1739, remembered the chapel being in a ruinous state, with only the east window remaining

Taxes were levied on such exported goods as wool, cloth and leather, and consequently, for centuries smuggling in Cornwall was mainly on out-going goods. To counter this, in 1401, Polperro had its first resident Customs men. The King's Council in London ordered that Thomas Curteys of Polperro and John Moyle of Looe were to be appointed "To warn all persons who they think fit that they must stop ships with a capacity to carry thirty tons or more from leaving port until clearance by the King." Robert Stephens of Polperro became the earliest-named smuggler and, when his ship was wrecked after many journeys to Ireland without paying dues, he was summoned to London.

The antiquary John Leyland rode round the country between 1534 and 1543 and from his pen we have the first visual description of Polperro:

"By Est the Haven of Fowey apon IIII Myles ys a smawle Creke cawled Poul Pier, and a symple and poore village (a litle fischar Toun) apon the Est Syde of the same of Fisshar Men and the Bootes ther Fisshing be saved by a Peere or Key."

A further description came in 1602, when Richard Carew of Anthony, a guest of Sir William Bevill of Killigarth Manor, wrote in his Survey of Cornwall:

"A little to the westward from Killigarth the poor harbour and village of Polperro there coucheth between the steep hills where plenty of fish is vented to the fish drivers whom we call jowters."

In 1833, E.W.Rashleigh of Kilmar, Par, described the piers:

"In Polperro is a sight that can be seen nowhere else. There are three piers. The first pier is now two hundred years old. It is built on wooden piles driven in after the manner of houses built in Venice, and the stone pier built on top. The stones immediately on the piles are very large and without any mortar or cement, so the sea plays right through the pier. It is built with a perfectly upright side facing the sea. The next pier was built about 1740. The side next to the sea is on a slant; it is on a rock foundation and built with mortar, no rubbish being used inside it. The modern pier, which is the outside one, is built with a curved surface to the sea and filled in with rubbish, with a cement end to it in the bottom."

THE FISHERMEN AT WORK

From time immemorial, pilchards have moved in quantity to feed off the Cornish coast and many writers have described the technique of pilchard fishing, but it was Jonathan Couch who first identified the fish as a large sardine, and drew Polperro fishermen at work. When fishing was under way, silence was essential to avoid disturbing the fish, so the master seaner gave the signal to take in the nets by waving his hat. The second boat, known as the 'lurker', was rowed by four men and showed the sean boat the area to be enclosed by nets. The sean boat had seven men on board, four rowing and three to shoot the nets, a process taking less than three minutes.

Pilchards were preserved in massive quantities in buildings called pallaces. Pallace Court, above the slip, was once such a building and in 1792 Jane Pearce leased the Old Pallace on the quay, which Zephaniah Job later rebuilt as the Pier Inn. Another pallace stood at Kit Hill, and in these buildings, for three shillings a night, women salted fish

The catch is landed.

and packed them up against the walls until a solid bulk three feet deep and six feet high was raised. After a month had elapsed, the fish were packed in hogsheads and the contents were pressed by heavy weights so the oil and salt seeped into specially made drains from which this 'train oil' was collected for use as nightlights, or sold for use in the preparation of leather. Even before 1800, Polperro's pilchards were sold far and wide, including three ports in Italy. Later, in the 20th century, two Italians - the Teglio brothers - settled in Polperro and leased the fish store below Pallace Court from where they exported to their home country. By the 1800s, the Cornish village was an established fishing port, depending on the pilchard to pay its way. Its inhabitants were ill-equipped to suffer setbacks to their industry.

Two terrible storms struck within seven years. In January 1817 the ruin was dreadful; out of 45 boats 30 were completely destroyed and others damaged almost beyond repair. The capital outlay for a boat was as much as for a house - John Rundle the shipwright lost his tools, timber and three boats under construction. Many houses were washed away, fish and salt stores were demolished and the old pier nearly destroyed as the sea surged over the Big Green, even stopping the mill wheel. Zephaniah Job had to rebuild the harbour damage at his own expense. Again, in November 1824, 19 boats were destroyed in a similar tempest, and the falling tide left the streets littered with debris.

Whole families were destitute. There was no social security, no family allowances, and the fishermen had to apply to the parish overseer for help from the inadequate poor rate. Before granting the destitute families any money, their children over ten years old had to be apprenticed to local farmers as domestic servants under the authority of magistrates.

Repairing a boat outside the old coastguard boathouse at the end of the 19th century.

Three generations at Troy Meadow, Polperro, more than one hundred years ago.

The village could look to no outside help, and Jonathan Couch realised that its whole future was in jeopardy. Ananiah Job had inherited the harbour from his uncle Zephaniah Job but in 1824 he could not afford to rebuild it and local landowners including Sir Harry Trelawny and the Bullers considered the ownership of the harbour facilities with its obligations for maintenance to be an unsafe investment and declined to buy the freehold. Couch is too modest a man to claim that his efforts saved the village and its fishing community but his long-unpublished account indicates all too clearly that his efforts started the recovery process.

Couch rode around the countryside, calling on clergy and landowners to acquaint them with Polperro's dire straits, and he called a meeting at the Ship Inn on 18th December 1824. A fund was raised to pay for new fishing boats, but they would also need the protection of new harbour walls. Eventually, Thomas Robins of Landaviddy and Nicholas Kendall undertook the rebuilding on condition that they were assigned inheritance of the harbour, piers and the Peak. There were many wearisome quarrels and mismanagements because this arrangement proved to be unsatisfactory, with the result that Couch went several times by coach to London to try to persuade the Admiralty that a committee of local people acting as trustees should be elected. It took exactly seventy years for the government to accept his proposals, by which time he was long dead. He had, however, managed to get the sanction of the Duchy of Cornwall to build the outer pier which had to be paid for by local people. Plans for this pier were drawn up by the Liskeard firm of Jenkins and Trathan, and the contractors Lang and Reed built it for five hundred pounds. The foundation stone was laid in 1861 amid much rejoicing.

Finally, in 1894, by Act of Parliament, an order was made incorporating the trustees of Polperro harbour, vesting it in them "for the improvement, maintenance and regulation of the port." The Act had the sanction of the Queen, but under all the Parliamentary verbiage, the local trustees had to pay all the costs incurred in buying the harbour rights, as well as preparing and obtaining the order. In those days the British government did not spend taxpayers' money if it could be avoided. so it was left to Polperro itself to raise the money required, by donations, fairs and bazaars, just as the villagers had done in 1391 to raise funds for the chapel on the Peak.

The new trustees issued a schedule of rates on vessels using the harbour and long list of charges for goods shipped, unshipped or transhipped. At that time, practically everything that was needed in the way of food, drink, clothes, farm animals and building materials all came by sea. It cost 3d to land a bed, 2d for a wheelbarrow, toys in boxes 1d a cubic foot. The landing dues on 108 gallons of ale was 1s, on 84 gallons of rum 2s, 4d for a gross of mineral waters and 1d for a dozen bottles of pickles. Everything was listed: asses, mules, poultry (2d a dozen birds), brooms, brushes, cakes. candles, cement, chairs, seeds, barley, flour.... The charge for landing salt, used in the curing of fish was 3d a ton, and to export a cask of pilchards weighing 476 lbs it cost 6d, a trunk or portmanteau under 28lbs paid 2d, writing slates 3d a gross and books 4d a hundredweight.

There was also a set charge for the use of cranes, weighing machines and sheds, and every vessel laid up in the harbour was charged 6d a year for each foot of keel. No boat making regular use of the port was to pay less than five shillings a year, and every pleasure boat entering the harbour paid one penny.

Lansallos and Talland Churches

Following the Norman conquest, Lansallos church was built on the venerated Celtic monastic site where the body of a female saint, St Hyldren, is said to lie. It is the 'lan' of a now unknown person and its old Cornish name was Lansalwys. Some of the Norman stone of the 11th century was used to build the new church in 1321 which was also dedicated to a female saint - St Ildierna. In the 14th century the rector for many years was Guy Blanchminster, whose sister Alice married Sir Richard Huish of Raphael Manor, who died in 1369. Effigies of Sir Richard and Alice now lie crumbling to dust in a dark corner of the church. Sir Richard was a knight in the service of the Black Prince and fought at the famous victory of Poitiers in 1356. He and his wife lay in recumbent state until their tomb was demolished, when they were buried under flagstones and found again in the restoration of the church which took place in 1884. In 1348, Alice Huish inherited one of the greatest treasures in English literature from her father, Sir Ralph Blanchminster. This was 'Brut', the first English language book to deal with the exploits of Arthur, champion of the Britons. What happened to this priceless treasure is unknown - only two copies survive and both are in the British Museum.

Fixed to the wall of the south aisle in Lansallos church is a fine slate engraving of Margery Budockshide who died in 1579. She wears a ruff, a stiff, brocaded gown with full sleeves, a tall hat with a veil and carries gloves and a prayer book. Her husband died abroad after an adventurous life which included fighting in Hungary against the Turks. There are some fine carved bench ends with human and arabesque scrolls, and the tombstones in Lansallos churchyard are a positive mine of information for those tracing their ancestors.

Ancient Talland church has one of the most beautiful settings in Cornwall. Its name means the 'lan on the brow' and its 13th century tower was built apart from the church but connected to it by a wagon-roof porch and a cobblestone floor. In about 1200, the Augustinian Priory of Launceston assumed ownership of the church, but later it became the responsibility of the owners of Killigarth Manor, who were successively the families of Beare, Bevill, Grenville, Hallett, Kendall, Gundry and Gundry Mills.

An early photograph of Talland church.

The unfortunate repairs and alterations of 1849-50 totally altered the interior - the handsome family pew presumably given by Sir Bernard Grenville was mutilated and all the woodwork shuffled about. The prayer desk, clerk's desk and pulpit - the latter of the James I period and known as a three-decker - were cut down and some of the panels used as bench ends. These unusual finials or tops seem to represent the clergy conducting different parts of the service, and the master-craftsmen who carved them gave the priests wings to show that they were God's messengers. One is holding a chalice, another is blessing something - perhaps bread - while another is reading from a scroll representing the Old Testament and the fourth reads from a book - the New Testament. But the great blaze of colour that once covered the walls is gone for ever. The medieval frescos depicted Christ on the cross, a group of mourning women, a Roman soldier, devil imps and monsters all painted in black, a sad man, a grinning dwarf and farm labourers at work. Other elements in these curious pictures included a four-masted sailing ship flying the flag of St Andrew and about to collide with a barred prison. According to Dr Box of Looe, writing in 1850, the effect was both novel and absurd.

The magnificent Bevill tomb chest shows Sir John Bevill, who died in 1579, in a fanciful suit of patterned armour with a long sword and dagger. In the Muster Roll of 1567 he provided the arms and armour for the Polperro and Talland men at the time when all able-bodied men between the ages of 16 and 60 had to attend the musters three times a year, to be trained to answer the call to arms at times of threatened invasion. This list shows the names of families still with descendants in the Polperro area, such as Oliver, Dyer, Minards, Couch, Libby, Hoskin, Searle, Gerry and Coode.

Then, their arms were bows and arrows, bills and pikes and some of them must have seen the Spanish Armada when the Spanish fleet was off Lansallos, sailing up the Channel to almost complete destruction.

Another fine slate figure in the church is that of Jane Mellow, who died in 1628, when giving birth to a son. It shows a woman sitting up in a fine four-poster bed wearing a cap and ruff and holding her infant son wrapped in an embroidered swaddling bag.

Tudor administrators used the ecclesiastical parishes as units of civil administration and the farm tenants had to serve as constables, church wardens and overseers of the poor - they kept order and shared their many duties. It was a harsh time, but some surviving parish accounts show compassion and humanity, in the form of charity bestowed upon the hordes of destitute persons passing through the Polperro area on their way to their own parishes:
1718.
Poor disbanded soldiers and seamen - 4s 8d
To a man whose house was burned - 1s 6d
To two lame men - 1s
To three wounded seamen and two women - 1s 6d
To six seamen who were cast away - 2s
Gave to a woman with four children - 6d

According to the churchwardens' accounts, there used to be a singing gallery in the church:
1775.
5s to Mr Winal for drawing the draft and measuring ground to build singing seats.
1778
Mr Jn. Winal finished singing seats, paid £20

Happily, this tradition of singing still continues and the fame and excellence of the Polperro Fishermen's Choir is well known in Cornwall and far beyond.

Between 1713 and 1747, Richard Doidge was Vicar at Talland church, and famous locally for ghost laying. His powers over the spirits of darkness were much respected, although his hold over his parishioners - many of whom were actively engaged in smuggling - was less sure for they did not always pay full heed to Doidge's sermons preached from his three-decker pulpit. He did not always live in the Parsonage House, being invited to reside at Killigarth by the Kendalls, thus leaving the churchyard as a convenient transit site for smuggled cargoes which had been run in on Talland sands. In 1745 Doidge wrote to the Bishop of Exeter, telling him there were two charity schools at Polperro - one supported by the interest on £100 given by Mary Kendall "for ye teaching of about 10 poore girls belonging to ye pish of Talland to read." Mary, of Killigarth Manor, is buried in Westminster Abbey. She deserves a place of honour in the history of Polperro - her interest in educating girls puts her in the position of being a full century and a half before her time.

JOHN WESLEY COMES TO POLPERRO
John Wesley came twice to preach in Polperro, and in his Journal he wrote:
"1762, Wednesday September 1st. I came about two to Polperro, a little village, four hours ride from Plymouth passage, surrounded with high mountains. However, abundance of people had found their way thither. And so had Satan too; for an old grey-headed sinner was busily cursing all the Methodists, just as we came into town. However, God gave his blessing, both to us and the congregation."

By 1900, when this photograph was taken, Wesleyan Methodism was strongly rooted in Polperro and there was even a school for children.

The great Methodist's second visit to Polperro was in September 1768 and he preached in John Rommett's house in the Warren, where he was invited to stay for the night, but Rommett's house smelled so strongly of pilchards and conger-eels that he gratefully accepted Mrs Martin's invitation to stay at their house on Talland Lane. John Rommett, a devout Methodist, was a fisherman and fish curer, and for many years his house was the meeting place and other preachers often stayed there. His house was too small for the growing numbers and Zebedee Minards and Richard Couch helped finance the building of the first Methodist Meeting House. This was opened in 1792 and had a provision for 250 people - the men sitting on one side and the women on the other.

Some of Lewis Harding's photographs of Polperro fishermen.

18

Zephaniah Job and the smugglers

In the 18th and 19th centuries, Britain was at war with France, Spain, America and Holland. Not surprisingly the duty on food and drink was high - sugar paid 30s a hundredweight, salt 15s a bushel, beer 10s a barrel, tea was taxed at no less than 96%, depending on its value per weight pound. Soap, candles, leather - even sailcloth was taxed.

And, in 1792 wages were not equal to such harsh duties. Local masons and carpenters received 2s a day, and many unskilled men and women in the village were employed loading ships, weeding or digging potatoes for just 6d a day. Consequently, it was hardly surprising that smuggling became vital to the economic life of a small community like Polperro. "All joined in it," wrote Jonathan Couch, "the smith left his forge, and the husbandman his plough; even women and children turned out to assist in the unlawful traffic, and received their share of the proceeds.... the gentry of the neighbourhood bought their brandy and lace; the excise and customs house officers connived at unlawful acts and profited by secret connections with the smugglers. Revenue cruisers were not infrequently detected with contraband goods on board and sometimes caught in the act.... the old and infirm were helped by the smugglers who brought in goods for sale without charging passage."

THE RISE OF ZEPHANIAH JOB

To be successful, smuggling had to be properly organised. Ships had to be properly loaded and unloaded, usually in the winter with no lights - and to land a cargo in Lantivet Bay or on Talland sands in foul weather can have been no easy task. Horses had to be hired from the farms and brought to the right place at the right time to clear cargoes before daylight.

The man who came to manage this business side of Polperro's smuggling industry - for that is what is was - was Zephaniah Job, who was born in St Agnes in Cornwall and who had fled to Polperro after a fight. His coming changed the life of the village - for he was to become the greatest single benefactor in its long history, Over the years, Job helped a large number of Polperro people by managing their financial affairs to enable them to save enough money to buy the freehold of their rented farms and houses at the break-up of Raphael Manor in 1813. For years, he was advisor, accountant and banker for many people. He hired lawyers in Liskeard and London when Polperro smugglers were to appear in court; he sent money or took it personally to them when they were in prison; he was steward of the manor of Raphael - responsible for the collection of rent and the renewal of leases. He was banker and business manager for the gentry too - for the whole Trelawny family in fact, paying their household bills at Trelawne, the school bills for the children at Westminster, Sir Harry's taxes on hair powder and the window tax for the manor house. Frequently, Sir Harry Trelawny borrowed very considerable sums of money from Job and his smuggling clients. No man would accept Sir Harry's signature on an IOU unless it was counter-signed by Job - despite the fact that Sir Harry was an ordained clergyman, a Justice of the Peace and a baronet!

Job also took charge of the pilchard export trade between Polperro and Italy, until it was ended by Napoleon. He was a corn trader, seed merchant, coal importer, he leased lime kilns in the Warren, Looe and Shallowpool; he was a timber merchant and he brought linen from Ireland to sell in Looe. And all this trade was carried out in his own sea-going barges sailing from Cattedown in Plymouth.

He kept a copy of every letter he wrote and his meticulous accounts balance to half a penny. Except for Sundays, he worked for every day in the year - with one exception. His exquisitely written letter book shows his quill pen was laid down on 24th December and taken up again on 26th December. He kept accounts for several ships which were fitted out as privateers between 1777 and 1815 - these were privately owned craft licenced by the Admiralty to attack and capture enemy ships. His main clients were the Quiller and Rowett families whose contributions to Britain's war efforts can hardly be equalled. They were magnificent seamen and are credited with the capture of eight enemy vessels, for which they received large sums of prize money. Job's accounts show they invested it wisely, building new houses and educating not only their sons but their daughters too.

THE INTRICACIES OF THE SMUGGLING TRADE

Zephaniah Job issued his own Polperro banknotes printed for him by Alderman Christopher Smith of London, but Job always observed the essential condition of having a coin fund available in exchange for his paper money. A note made by Jonathan Couch in 1823 - a year after Job's death - gives an idea of how local Cornish banks worked:

"We shall probably never see anything like them again. They had their origin in the paper money system, which began in the French Revolution, and scarcely a town was without one. There was one at Fowey which ended in bankruptcy, two at Liskeard .... one at Polperro which ended in Mr Job's death. He left a good fortune to his administrators...."

Job was strict with his clients and insisted that they pay for their goods "at the ready money price whether lost or

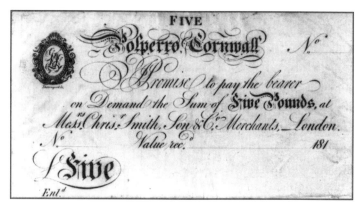

The Polperro five pound note, issued by Zephaniah Job

not" and 'lost' in this sense meant taken by the revenue cutters or customs men. A letter, dated April 1795, to a Guernsey wine merchants told them that Richard Rowett in the *Happy Return* had been taken by a revenue cutter after a chase lasting twenty eight hours, and "indeed the risk is now very great for these small boats," he wrote. "I would advise them to do very little in the summer months when there is such a look out." More bad news was to follow:

Messrs Peter de Lisle & Sons   Polperro. 20 May 1795
    Gentlemen,
    I duly received your esteemed favour of the 5th with the note of Robert Mark, John Mark, John Barrett for £64.0s.6d and am very sorry they were unfortunate as to fall a prey to the Greyhound cutter which they held too cheap supposing it to be a King's cutter depending on the sailing of their own. They stood too near the cutter. I have repeatedly told them it is never good to hold an adversary too cheap.

I have to profer you my thanks for an anker of gin, you were so obliging to send me tho' I have not yet had the good fortune to recover it, your friendly intentions is the same. I hope I shall have it in my favour to make you some returns for your favour and friendship...."

When the Polperro privateers were at sea on behalf of the government, they seemed to have combined official business with their own personal and private enterprises. They collected cargoes of liquor and dry goods from Guernsey and the usual procedure was for Job to guarantee his clients by name to the Guernsey merchants with whom he dealt. After the smuggled goods had been sold, they paid Job in cash and he transferred the money to his London agent Christopher Smith, who made the final transfer to the Channel Islands. The contraband originated in France, and was shipped to Guernsey where the Cornishmen collected when they could. The French government was well aware of the illicit trade and was only too happy to deprive the British government of revenue.

One entry in Job's book for 1795 reads as follows:
William Johns - £3,760
John Langmaid - £629
Richard Rowett - £1,020
Rowett, Langmaid & Willcocks Jn. - £347
John Clements & Co. - £309
Barrett, Mark & Co. - £1,503
Robert Rean - £1,200

These sums show only the wholesale cost of goods as Job kept no records of the profits made by his clients, nor is there any indication as to who bought the vast quantities

View of Polperro about 1900, looking towards the Coombs

of smuggled goods and liquor, In modern money terms, something like the equivalent of a million pounds passed through Job's books, and that doesn't include the ton of other books known to have been burnt. The total figures involved, therefore, are impossible to estimate. Job's charges seem to have been no more than half of 1%, which he raised to 1% in 1783.

A typical entry reads:

"To the writing of an infinite number of letters - 1 guinea."

Captured contraband was frequently advertised for sale:

"Port of Looe - 6th June 1800.
By order of the Honorable Commissioner of H.M. Customs on Friday the 20th day of this instant June by two o'clock in the afternoon will be exposed for PUBLIC SALE at the Customs House in this port in several lots and sold to the highest bidder.
The goods undermentioned viz:
Brandy - 959 gallons, Rum - 144 gallons, Geneva -1003 gallons"

After 1800, the government began to take sterner action against smuggling and Polperro was the first port where men of the newly organised Preventive Water Guard Service were stationed "For the suppressing of smuggling and outrage, the preservation of life and prosperity from shipwreck and of service for the Defence of the Nation." In 1801 the preventive boat sailed into Polperro harbour, and it is easy to picture the consternation of Zephaniah Job and his fellow conspirators as they watched it lower sail and make fast to the quay. The vessel was based in the port for years, but, surprisingly, seems to have led an inactive life, it being said that none of its crew had died in service.

Job turned his energies to other enterprises. When Sir Jonathan Phillipps of Launceston, owner of Raphael Manor, died leaving an infant son, the trustees of the estate decide to sell up. Every property on the estate had been previously held on life leases, but now by Act of Parliament - the Phillipps Estate Act of 1813 - for the first time in 700 years anyone could buy the property freehold. George Coath of Penhellick in Pelynt bought the manor house itself for £3,000, Thomas Robins of Liskeard bought and rebuilt Landaviddy and Job himself paid £630 for 17 properties in Polperro. But the storm of 1817 destroyed much of Job's new property and making good the damage left him much less prosperous than before.

Because of his singular name and his great influence on his home village, Zephaniah Job has attracted a good deal of comment, much of it inaccurate. He never lived at present-day Crumplehorn Mill, nor did he print counterfeit banknotes there. For the last 20 years of his life he leased Great Kellow in Lansallos from the Bullers of Morval. He died "at a dwelling house, situated at Crenible Horn in Lansallos", having never married and without making a will. His nephew Ananiah Job, son of his brother John, inherited the harbour. In his last illness, Job, aged 75, was attended by Jonathan Couch - then aged 33 - whose account came to £12.13s.6d. The cash in Job's house on the day after his death amounted to a staggering £1,442.19s.1d and all the notes on the Polperro bank were honoured and paid on application.

Smuggling continued long after his death, but inevitably the old ways changed and, by the mid 1850s more than 50 Polperro men had 'joined the other side' and were serving in the Royal Navy and the Coastguard. It was now the ambition of many men and boys to join the services their grandfathers hated and feared.

A fine study of part of the fishing fleet in harbour at low tide, sometime in the 1880s.

Jonathan Couch 1789-1870
Surgeon Apothecary of Polperro

Jonathan Couch: An early portrait, dated about 1855.

Jonathan Couch was born in Polperro on 11th March 1789, in the house in the Warren now called Warren Cottage. His contribution to scientific knowledge is impressive by any standard, for besides being a hard-working doctor and apothecary, riding miles on his horse 'old Grey' to visit patients, he was a classical scholar reading and writing Latin and Greek, a zoologist, ichthyologist, botanist and archaeologist.

He was educated at the Dame School in Polperro, where he learned to read from a horn book. This was a rectangular oak board with a short handle on which was placed the lesson card or ABC, covered by transparent horn. For more than three hundred years children learned to read from such books, which, in fact, were not books at all. Couch's later education, at Lansallos and Bodmin Grammar School, paved the way to study at medical schools in London, during which he was profoundly influenced by the men under whom he studied, who included some of the best men in their fields. He returned to Polperro in 1810 and applied his newly acquired surgical skills to the dissection and study of the fish so vital to the welfare of his village. At that time, knowledge about the life of fish was sparse indeed. For example, no one knew what the John Dory fed on, and as this fish was then regarded as good food for the table, Couch thought it important to establish its feeding cycles. As he dissected the fish he made hundreds of drawings of their bones and joints and in his study he had a special stand which held each fish while a jet of water played over it so that he could paint the fresh brilliance before the colours faded. He relied on knowledgeable and experienced local fishermen to help him in his research and his home in Lansallos Street was always busy with the comings and goings on men and boys bringing in seaweed, fish scales, crabs, lobsters, shells and jellyfish. The scene was described many years later by his famous grandson, Sir Arthur Quiller Couch. A fictitious Mrs Puckey is addressing the doctor:

"And your 'natomies and fish innards may be all very well, and tell the men to wipe their sea boots 'pon the front mat. When it comes to their unpicking a trawl in your very drawing room, an' fish scales all over the best Brussels as I've a-see'd em before now...."

One of his exquisite illustrations for his work on fishes.

A great deal of Couch's varied work was published during his lifetime, including articles on molluscs, Cornish zoophytes, the growth rate of crabs and lobsters (warning of the dangers of over-fishing), observations on the diseases of potatoes, on shooting stars, the midge fly that infects wheat, the habits of bats, the natural history of the salmon and the *Cornish Fauna*, published in 1838. Many of his observations were included in another book published in 1847 - *Illustrations of Instinct, deduced from the habits of British Animals*. He did not agree that the actions of man were governed by reason and those of animals by instinct, and communication between man and animals by sounds abnormal to both forms the basis for one chapter and was written a full century before modern scientific research under controlled conditions was made. His major work was *Fishes of the British Isles*, published in four volumes between 1862 and 1865. This great work contained 256 coloured water colours and drawings, all made by himself while the fish were still alive and not, as he said, disguised by imaginary adorning. The whole work is of considerable artistic merit as well as a major contribution to scientific knowledge.

In 1837 there was an outbreak of smallpox in Polperro and Couch inoculated 285 patients and vaccinated a further 150. The method he used was to dip ivory points in the lymph from the pustule of a person who had been vaccinated between five and eight days previously:

"All that were inoculated took the infection on the first application and all have done well. Some of the children had emaciated conditions and some disorders of the skin.... it was a greater trial than I ever saw before from this operation....."

At that time there was much opposition to any form of vaccination against smallpox - some thought it might bring on cow-like characteristics - but this episode demonstrates that Couch was in the forefront of medical opinion and practice and that virtually the whole of Polperro trusted their doctor to do something that even Parliament was uncertain about - a great vote of confidence in the man.

"Trust yourself to th' old Doctor and he'll see you come to a nat'ral end o' some sort, and in no haste neither."

Jonathan Couch was a man of middle height and always immaculately dressed, keeping to the fashion of George IV's time, wearing the double white neckerchief fashionable in his youth. His suits were made in London, a traveller from his tailor coming to the village specially to take his measurements, and he habitually wore a tall, black stove pipe hat and shoes with broad silver buckles specially made for him out of crown pieces by Sam Coad the blacksmith. Lanes in and out of Polperro were too steep and muddy for the use of a horse-drawn vehicle so Couch rode or walked and, according to his son Thomas, was not averse to wading through snowdrifts to reach his patients.

He married three times. His first marriage was brief, his wife Jane dying in childbirth and his second, in 1815, was to Jane Quiller, one of the twin daughters of Richard Quiller. When Jane's mother died, they moved into the Quiller home which became known as Couch's House, and still is today. They had six children, and three sons - Richard, Thomas and John - became doctors in Bodmin and Penzance and bore their mother's name, Quiller. Richard was involved in one of the greatest discoveries in Cornish geology. In 1841, he

and Charles W. Peach found a magnificent fossil fish bed at Scilly Cove, lying exposed and undiscovered by geologists. They made other finds at Giggan Cove, Lake Rock, Talland and Rotterdam beach. Richard also found tree remains of oak and beach exposed on Polperro beach. "The whole of the hills," he wrote, "as well as the valleys, must once have formed the bottom of the seas, then elevated to allow the growth of large trees, then all submerged to a great extent." He had found the submarine forest which is today shown on Ordnance maps.

Jonathan Couch was 70 at the time of his third marriage, but he new wife, a local girl named Sarah Lander Roose, was just 22. Polperro chattered with surprise. In 1870, the venerable doctor died peacefully in his sleep. 'Q' described him as "a patient man of science who spent his life observing the habits of fish, without attempting to teach the Almighty how to improve them."

The ancient mills

Between the 13th and 20th centuries there were at least seven water mills in the Polperro area, making cloth and grinding corn, the last two to survive being Manor Mill in Polperro itself and Killigarth Manor Mill (now called Crumplehorn Mill). Others were at Old Mill Cove, below Hendersick Farm, which dated from 1251; Tresquite Mill which made cloth and was mentioned as long ago as 1199; and Kellow or Long Coomb Mill, dating from the 13th century - the last-named being a 'fulling' mill, this being a process of cleaning and thickening wool by washing and pounding it. The place name Wool Washing also indicates an early site of industry in Long Coomb, where activity didn't cease until the 19th century.

The Talland Mill of 1411 was washed into the sea about two hundred years ago and only its leat survives today, but sometime before 1600 it was the scene of a daring kidnapping. Joan, the daughter of John Tallan, married John Morth, who had in his employ a Breton miller. This man returned to France when war broke out, but, on Christmas night returned in a French-manned vessel and headed for Talland Mill. The family were dining when the gang broke in and "carried the guests speedily to Lanjreghey and forceth the gent to redeem his enlargement with the sale of a great part of his revenues." In modern parlance, ransom was demanded.

The horse bus at Crumplehorn Mill, photographed by Lewis Harding around 1850.

THE WORKING OF THE MILLS

The water wheel was a triumph of medieval technology, and the miller an important man in any community. When the landowners, starting with the Normans, built their mills, the capital outlay and cost of upkeep would have been prohibitive unless enough grain could be supplied to keep them in full operation, and so every tenant had the obligation to use their lord's mill written into their life leases. Even as late as the mid-1800s it was still customary to take local wheat to local mills to be ground. Polperro housewives baked their loaves by placing the well kneaded dough on the hearth stone and covering it with an earthenware pot which was then buried in the embers of the fire. But progress was to have curious side effects. Fireplaces in many of the older homes had very wide chimneys suitable only for the burning of wood and when coal was imported direct from Wales, in the early 19th century, these chimneys were walled up and the hearths made smaller and more suitable for the burning of coal. Consequently, bread could no longer be baked in the home and so three new bakehouses opened and soon did very well. One such bakehouse was in the Warren, one at the Noughts and Crosses and the third at the Mill House itself. Dinners were also cooked at these houses, for a halfpenny a time, and this custom continues today - many turkeys being baked in Jack Joslin's Bake House. A delectable aroma fills Polperro's narrow streets when the ovens open and people hurry home with their Christmas dinners.

In 1891, Henry Wright of St Neots took over Manor Mill. He set out early in the morning of March 9th to walk to his new home with his ten year old son and a young bullock. Snow began to fall. The great blizzard of 1891, which passed into legend, had begun.

The boy stepped in his father's footsteps until at last they reached Polperro and slept, exhausted, in a barn. It was this boy, William Henry Wright, who later built the present Mill House, now a guest house. In 1915 he went to war, returning in 1918, but not to start the mill wheel turning again for it was no longer a paying proposition to grind in the old way. The wheel lay still for over ten years, until the greatest domestic revolution in mankind's history - electricity - came to Polperro. The ancient mill then became the electric power station.

About 1929, Sir George Hussey and two friends, who spent their holidays in Polperro, formed a company to provide the village with electricity and the wooden mill wheel was removed and replaced with a turbine wheel to generate current to light the streets, and, even more important for the fishermen, to power an ice-making plant. Thus, Manor Mill spans the gap between the most important mechanical invention of the medieval world and the greatest modern domestic development. Perhaps when the fossil fuels run out, the water wheels of medieval Polperro will turn again.

The Calender Customs

The social occasions of rural communities were already established long before Christianity and centred around the seasons of the year - the two great European festivals taking place at the winter solstice - Yule-tide or mid-winters day on 21st December, when all rejoiced as the days lengthened - and mid-summer when the days declined as the sun touched the Tropic of Cancer. Until the 18th century, many Polperro folk rose early on Easter Day to see "the sun dance" - but this pagan custom is shrouded in mystery.

The Polperro Goosey Dancers, by long custom, were allowed to go uninvited into any house, walking miles to act out their play and then vanish again into the winter night. At Christmas 1872 the 'Guise Dancers' or 'Goosey Dancers' invaded Trenant near Looe and petrified Hester Peel who did not understand why a crowd of strangers dressed as St George, the Devil, a doctor and a group of soldiers should invade her privacy late at night. But the people were merely carrying out a ritual which is so old it is believed to date from pagan Rome, but which continued in the Polperro area up until a mere century ago.

Boys and girls, too, borrowed clothes and disguised themselves so well that it was impossible to recognise them, and it was considered churlish to take offence at anything they said. Like the Goosey Dancers, they were allowed to enter any home to dance and sing and to eat and drink as they pleased - and so deeply was this custom embedded in local tradition that, despite being obviously pagan in origin, it was allowed to continue even in the stern Victorian age. The Christmas or Yule-tide play was also performed by children, in a fish cellar or at an inn, and the proceedings were always opened by Father Christmas and his page:

Here come I, Old Father Christmas,
Welcome, or welcome not
I hope Old Father Christmas
Will never be forgot.

LEFT: A group of Polperro folk gathered outside the Three Pilchards Inn on the right. Photographed by Lewis Harding about 1860.

This was followed by a Turkish knight shouting loudly against St George, who then appeared fully armed, to confront him, and in the ensuing battle the Turk was vanquished and a doctor summoned to "Tend this deep and deadly wound". This was done using elecampane, a herb of ancient medicinal repute mentioned in Anglo-Saxon writings and grown in Elizabethan physic gardens. Despite this medication, the Turk died and his body was removed by a hobby-horse. A dragon then appeared, belching real fire and smoke from his snout, and often the actors were burned in the cause of the ritual before the beast was finally overcome by good St George.

The Polperro midsummer bonfire - painted by H.E.Butler

The Polperro fair was always held on the 10th July, when a huge bonfire of tar barrels and wood was built on the beach. Men and boys danced around it singing, and next day the fair began in earnest and lasted for several days. Stalls were set up in Lansallos Street and around the harbour, the vendors selling toys, sweets, gifts and ribbons. Crowds came from miles around, strolling players performed tragic and comic plays, ballad singers performed in the streets and the gaberlunzie man sold little bundles of sulphur matches. One year, a German band came to play, for several years a bear shambled down the hill terrifying children, and the penny-peep men did a brisk trade acting out scenes from the latest murder with gruesome relish and there were wrestling matches and rowing contests

On the last day of St Peter's Fair, there was the ceremony of Mock Mayor. Someone dressed in absurd clothes, bearing a passing resemblance to the Mayor of Looe, chose his constables with drunken dignity and then rode into town in a jowter's cart decorated with greenery. Progressing slowly, they stopped at each inn, where the Mayor made numerous speeches promising better wages, better times ahead and free beer all the year round. He was then tipped into the sea.

Another popular form of public ridicule was 'The Riding'. A couple accused of immorality were punished by the sight of two people in a donkey cart, dressed to resemble themselves. Grim retribution attended this ceremony in 1836 when a procession of men and boys acted as trumpeters, providing an escort for the cart and following it down to the harbour. Instead of trumpets they blew on the instruments which doubled as bullock horns and fog horns. The noisy procession paraded through the streets to the quay, where someone loaded one of the old cast iron cannon which had stood at the entrance since the end of the war in 1815. When fired, it blew up, badly injuring one Thomas Broad in the knee and thigh. The Riding never took place again. It mocked the breaking of the most important contract in both primitive and advanced societies - marriage. The marriage ceremony seems to have always been a public one, indicating the interest and approval of the whole community. As anyone living in Polperro will know, it is a very long walk to either of the parish churches, and in the 19th century the "Walking Wedding" had a ritual of its own. The bride's father was the first to leave, and he walked alone, dressed in white duck trousers, a blue coat, a high hat and white gloves, and usually he carried in his hand a piece of bread or cake which he gave to the first person he met along the way. This gift was called a kimbly. Then the bride left home with the best man and two bridesmaids, and when they were on their way the bride's mother, accompanied by the bridegroom, left, to be followed by the rest of the wedding party two by two. Sometimes, at the top of the hill, farm wagons decked in greenery were waiting to take the party on to church, and when all returned boats in the harbour were dressed overall with flags, and volleys were fired from pistols, fowling pieces and muskets. Then came the wedding feast, after which the couple went home - the honeymoon is a modern invention - and the groom went to work the next day as normal.

The giving of cake or bread on the way to church must have had some long-forgotten significance, because Polperro boys often sang to a bat as it flew overhead:

Airey mouse, airey mouse, fly over my head,
And you shall have a crust of bread;

And when I brew and when I bake
You shall have a piece of my wedding cake.

Cornwall and Brittany had similar ceremonies on "Hall Monday" - the day before Shrove Tuesday. Nicky-Nan-Night, or Nic-Nan-Neuf, was the night when boys hammered doors with clubs as they ran through the streets singing:

Nicky nicky nan
Give me some pancake, then I'll be gone
But if you give me none
I'll throw a stone
And down your door will come.

Another custom which continued in Polperro until the early part of the 19th century was the making of a figure of straw and dressing it in old clothes. The dummy was carried through the streets amidst much laughter and taken to the beach where it was methodically shot at, stoned and finally burnt to ashes. On Good Fridays there was a fair at Mable Barrow when standings (stalls) were set up to sell jam pasties, and after the meal there were games and dancing to the music of harmonicas and concertinas. Mable Barrow, of course, is a Bronze Age burial mound and, moreover, a long way from either parish church. One can only speculate why the Christian festival was celebrated at such a place. Also on Good Friday, Polperro folk set out to walk to Looe Island, which could be reached across the sands at low tide, taking hot-cross buns to sustain them on the journey. Such buns were also sometimes hung up on a string till the following year, and, according to Thomas Quiller Couch, they were grated into a warm mash and used to tend sick cattle or children.

May Day was a great public holiday. In Polperro, all rose early and went 'a-maying' to gather leaves and flowers. Elm boughs and whitethorn were gathered and then boys with buckets, cans, bottles, anything that would hold water, were allowed to drench anyone unless that person was 'protected' by a piece of may conspicuously displayed. To escape a soaking they had to sing: "The first of May is Dipping Day..."

Dancing around the maypole died an unnatural death in the Polperro area when the influential Buller family put an end to the ancient custom of allowing the people to cut down a tree to use as a pole. Some people thought the pole was "a stinckyn idol about which people leape and daunce, as the hethen did...."

A GREAT VICTORY CELEBRATED

After Nelson won the Battle of Copenhagen and General Abercrombie won the Battle of Alexandria, the Treaty of Amiens was signed - only a truce as it turned out - but on the 24th October 1801, the *Royal Cornwall Gazette* reported that an order had been received at Portsmouth to pay off all the armed ships and hired cutters, and when this news came through Polperro went wild with joy:

"Amid all the effusions of joy which have on late been so publickly shown throughout the country on the Ratification of the Preliminaries of Peace at Polperro in this county, such unbounded joy was diffused on news of this Ratification.... that an immediate illumination took place and even the smallest cot houses had their windows filled with light. To a spectator, from the amazing high hills which surround that little town, the sight was truly grand and sublime.... The manifestation of public joy did not stop there, for on the

succeeding night a large pile of combustibles was raised on the highest point of a hill, which must have been visible 18 or 20 leagues to sea; and was accompanied with such shouts of exultation and incessant firing, that the roaring of the sea was entirely drowned, in the popular clangor. After the bonfire was extinguished the principal inhabitants repaired to the Ship Inn where an elegant supper was prepared; and a variety of sentimental toasts with some excellent loyal songs, closed the festivity of the night."

The landlord of the Ship Inn in Fore Street at that time was Charles Guy who in 1800 caused a sensation by being given the first umbrella ever seen in the village. Couch relates with pleasure that: "when he walked the streets with it over his head, all eyes were turned on him as if some rare animal were there: while every looker-on joined in the exclamations of the pride of some folks, for their parts, they would have accepted it - but it should never have seen the light: they would have locked it away in their chests."

Decline, change and revival

There were to be many changes to the old way of life. Occupational changes followed economic changes - new work being found as old trades declined and decayed. When the centuries-old Polperro tradition of weaving - based in farmhouse and cottage - gradually died out, the women of the village turned to knitting. They produced knit frocks, then the only protection for fishermen long before the invention of the oil-skin, and guernseys and large quantities of stockings. At this time of great hardship, the wool was supplied by Plymouth merchants on the iniquitous truck or barter system - the knitters having to accept goods as

Excitement at the harbour as a thrasher shark is landed, probably in the year 1854

payment whether they wanted them or not. Many Polperro women walked to Plymouth and back, carrying the finished garments or wool on their backs; on their feet they wore clogs, known as patterns, which had wooden soles ringed with iron to keep out the wet.

Occupations in the village were still varied. In 1851, for example, there were 47 fishermen, two sail makers, 19 knitters, 13 shoemakers, 11 dressmakers, one nurse, eight tailors, nine coastguards, 11 bonnet makers and one straw bonnet maker. Mrs Grace Pinch, aged 70, helped by her daughter Jane, ran a travellers' lodging house in Bevill Row - an early forerunner of the later guesthouses. The Ship, the Fisherman's Arms, the New Inn and the Three Pilchards took care of the drinking requirements of the inhabitants, although all were greatly opposed by the long-established Polperro teetotaller societies, who tried continuously to turn them all into temperance establishments. The matter came to a head in 1886, when Police Superintendent Barnes objected to all the inns and the case came before the Bench. The Chairman of that worthy body, however, was unable to decide which establishments to close and so, very wisely, ruled that all should stay open.

At the end of the 19th century boats were laid up, nets were rotting and many people were hungry in Polperro. The great shoals of pilchards upon which its prosperity still depended, had vanished as mysteriously as they had come. Young men left to find work up-country and overseas - farming collapsed and local landowners began to sell up because ownership no longer paid due to cheap American wheat and cheap Australian and Argentinian meat flooding the British markets. The balance of English society was being irrevocably changed for, to pay for this imported food, the country had to produce vast quantities of manufactured goods, and the tremors caused by the revolution were felt even in remote Polperro, where resident landowners such as the Trelawnys, sold their estates to industrial magnates like the Morleys - the stocking manufacturers - who bought Trelawne. In turn, many of the new owners soon sold these large houses because of a shortage of servants - the women preferring the better paid work in the industrial cities and towns.

Looe Island, Kellow, Penglaze, Tregue, Long Coomb Mill, Langreek, the Wesleyan Chapel at Crumplehorn and literally dozens of farms went up for sale over a period of years. Only eight years after the Gundry brothers bought, demolished and rebuilt old Killigarth House, both the new house and its manor farms had to be auctioned in 1878 at Webb's Hotel in Liskeard.

But all was not gloom and despondency, for great improvements and far-reaching developments were under way at the same time. Education had been available to the children of Polperro from a very early stage, as is proven by the very long-standing ability of Polperro men and women to read and write. The earliest school for boys had been supported by a gift from a Captain Kendall RN, and one of the Trelawny daughters donated land for the building of Sclerder Abbey, a girl's school for sixteen boarders run by nuns. In 1840, William Rawlings, Rector of Lansallos, started a free day school for one hundred boys of the Church of England denomination and Mrs Jane Rundle Hitchens, daughter of Jonathan Couch by his first marriage, taught the Wesleyan children. When Dr John Quiller Couch died at Penzance in 1900, he left £1,400 to be invested and the income was to be used for the education of Polperro children at Liskeard County School. His will stipulated there was to be no religious discrimination in the selection of these pupils and Couch Foundation trustees set examinations and allocated four scholarships a year for three years. It is pleasant to record that the good men do sometimes lives after them, for the Couch Foundation now allocates money to Polperro students at Technical College.

Not everyone in the village approved of all this book-learning. An old man, unfortunately anonymous, is recorded as saying:

"Eddication indeed! Eddication is the ruination of our country. 'Ere they be zetting down a playin'o' the muzick; better'n they'd be brought op to mak guid wives and zew and knett."

THE LOSS OF ISOLATION

Less than 200 years ago, the fastest a man could travel was the speed of a galloping horse. In 1800, there was one horse and cart in Lansallos parish, but the mobility of the locals was improved by 1851, when George Lord of Polperro had a horse bus 'The Speculator', and W. Tucker's similar vehicle ran from Crumplehorn a few years later. In 1900, Arthur Job's bus provided a service between Crumplehorn and the Tavistock Hotel in Devonport, with a regular van service twice daily to the new railway station at Looe. Visitors to Plymouth could use 'The Scarlet Runner' weekly horse bus, or the *Beatrice Annie* sailing vessel which plied between the harbour and Great Western Dock, in the same way that Zephaniah Job's trading barges had done a century earlier.

One of Job's descendants had bought Killigarth Mill, and in one of the out-buildings was to repose something which was to sweep away Polperro's isolation in a few short years. Thomas Job never used his new possession - the first licenced vehicle powered by an internal combustion engine using petrol was a 3 HP Armac motor cycle made in the USA and owned by Charles Boutwood of Hillside, Talland Hill. He registered it in 1907, and in 1912, Dr. Matthew Hutchinson of Lanhael became the first registered owner of a motor car, a two seater coupe with a dickey seat. The age of the motor car had small beginnings, but eventually the New Road into the village had to be resurfaced, and a mammoth steam roller belching fire is still remembered, as slowly, yard by yard, asphalt was laid over the surface.

In 1930, the Cornwall branch of the Council for the Preservation of Rural England made a recommendation about Polperro's traffic and one of the council members was Sir Arthur Quiller Couch:

"Fishing is still fortunately the main source of livelihood, but there is also increasing evidence of the caterers for tourist traffic. The Immense motor coaches that visit the place daily during the summer season seem totally alien to the atmosphere of the village. Yet the needs of the daily tripper must be considered; we can only suggest that a more spacious motor park should be provided outside the village and that visitors should walk to the harbour."

It took 38 years, until 1968, before local opposition was overcome and the car-park built, but no-one living or trading in Polperro today can be unaware of the immeasurable benefits the traffic ban has brought to the quality of life there.

A PLACE WITH A FUTURE

Today, despite the thousands of cars that park in the visitors' car-park at Long Coomb, sheep and cattle still graze on the green slopes above, as they have done since the Norman clerks making the Domesday survey in 1086 wrote down their numbers. Norse longboats once pillaged and burnt in the West Country, today Scandinavian refrigeration lorries take mackerel and shellfish back to the northlands, and our former foes - the French, the Dutch and the Germans - come in their thousands to holiday in Polperro.

Today's visitor to Polperro sees an irregular and colourful collection of stone-built houses, dating mainly from the 18th and 19th centuries, sturdily built of locally quarried stone and built to replace the earlier dwellings of clay and straw which have not survived the great tempests which so often sweep into the haven. The towering cliffs are spectacular and look solid enough, but a great deal of land on the seaward side of Polperro has vanished during the last two hundred years. A single roller of the Atlantic ground swell is estimated to fall with a pressure of a ton on every square foot of land, and winter waves fall with three times that force. The sea still dominates. For more than a thousand years it has brought sorrow, disaster, hardship and havoc - but it has also brought prosperity. Every winter, when the elements rage and the sea batters the coast and fishing boats lie storm-bound, it is not such an ill wind as it seems. The essential salts - the phosphates and nitrogen - are mixing in the turbulent waters, and when Spring comes the tiny animals of the plankton species drift helplessly in the surface waters and the sea off Polperro abounds with the larval stages of crustaceans, sea urchins, acorn barnacles, molluscs, all of which attract the surface-feeding fish like the mackerel and the pilchard - the fish on which Polperro's existence has always largely depended.

More recently, the Harbour Trustees have encouraged interest in Polperro's heritage by establishing the Museum of Smuggling and Fishing in a former pilchard factory in the Warren once owned by the Teglio brothers. The Museum now houses a remarkable collection of early photographs and other memorabilia dating back over 200 years to a time when both smuggling and fishing thrived in this extraordinary Cornish fishing village.

"The sea still dominates."

36